I AM A PRAYING KID

40 Simple Ways to Talk to GOD

warnerpress.org

30580PO100000041

Excerpts taken from *The Secret Weapon: Teaching Kids to Pray* by Tina Houser.

Edited by Robin Loisch

Design by Curtis D. Corzine

ISBN: 9781684346028

ALPHABET THANKFULNESS PRAYER

Devote yourselves to prayer with an alert mind and a thankful heart. Colossians 4:2 (NLT)

)n a sheet of paper, write down the letters of the alphabet. Jext to each letter, write something God made.

Everything comes from the hand of God. Something nay be made in a factory, but the "stuff" it's made of vas created by God. When you trace it back to its very eginning, God was there, making the ingredients!

Ve take so many things for granted, like blades of grass, he wind, an umbrella on a rainy day, and Band-Aids to over our scraped knees. Let's pay attention to things round us and thank God for them.

ook at the letters and words you wrote. Now say a prayer or each one: "Thank You, God, for ________ because they re ____________."

ALTAR PRAYER

> *Are any of you sick? You should call for the elders of the church to come and pray over you, anointing you with oil in the name of the Lord.*
> James 5:14 (NLT)

Does your church have an altar? It may look like a wooden kneeling bench and is usually near the front of the church sanctuary.

People come to the altar to pray about special needs. Maybe they have a problem and want to ask God for help. Maybe they want to pray for a friend or family member. Sometimes they ask God to forgive them for something wrong they have done. Some come to pray for healing.

The pastor or church members may pray with people at the altar. The pastor may anoint a person with oil. To anoint means "to set apart." When a person is anointed, their situation is set apart, and people focus their prayers on that one special need. There is no special power in the oil. It is a symbol of God's power.

Do you have a special need you want to pray about? You can kneel beside your bed or in front of your chair and make that place an altar to God.

BE A FRIEND PRAYER

Pray for one another so that you might be healed. The prayer of a godly person is powerful. Things happen because of it. James 5:16 (NIrV)

The Bible tells the story of a paralyzed man who was brought to Jesus by four friends. (Read Mark 2:1–12.) There was no way for them to get the man into the house where Jesus was because of the crowd, so they cut a hole in the roof and lowered the man down in front of Jesus. When Jesus healed the man, He said that it was the faith of the man's friends that made the man well.

Praying for your friends...having faith for your friends... is important! We pray so our friends will have their souls healed. Prayer is powerful and it makes things happen!

Talk to God about your friends who need to know Him. Ask God to make you a good example for them. Ask God to show you how you can help your friends to know Jesus.

BREATHING PRAYER

I can never escape from your Spirit! I can never get away from your presence! Psalm 139:7 (NLT)

What happens when we stop breathing completely? Maybe you have held your breath before when you took swimming lessons. What a relief it is to take a nice big breath when your head pops above water! Breathing is important, isn't it?

Praying is important too. Breathing and praying are alike Breathing keeps our bodies alive, and praying keeps our souls alive. God made our bodies so that they don't forget to breathe, but sometimes we do forget to pray. When we start forgetting to pray often, we get further and further away from God. It's as if we don't know Him anymore.

Through prayer we "inhale" God by coming into His presence. Praying should be as natural to a God-follower as breathing is, and much more satisfying! Pray often and keep breathing!

CHOP CHOP PRAYER

When you are tempted, God will give you a way out. Then you will be able to deal with it.
1 Corinthians 10:13 (NIrV)

Write down things that tempt you to turn away from God and keep you from spending time with Him.

Do you remember the Bible story about Samson? (Read Judges 13–16.) God gave Samson amazing strength as long as he didn't cut his hair. When Samson's hair was cut, his strength was gone. When he was tempted and told the secret of his strength, Samson broke his commitment to God. Samson was strong physically, but his commitment wasn't so strong.

Just like Samson, you must choose each day whether to stay strong in your commitment to God or to fall for Satan's temptations. Satan knows your weaknesses, and he will try to wear you down, just like he wore down Samson.

The good news is that God can give you new strength! When you admit to God that you've been tempted and have done wrong things, God forgives you. You can have a fresh start.

COVER ONE ANOTHER

The earnest prayer of a righteous person has great power and produces wonderful results.
James 5:16 (NLT)

Choose a paper clip and hold it in your hand. Give your paper clip the name of someone you want to pray for. James 5:16 says our prayers should be "earnest." That means we really, really mean what we are saying. We should cover our person with prayer—we should pray a lot, not just once a week.

When you place your hand over your paper clip (the person you are praying for), that represents how you are covering them in prayer. You pray for him or her in the morning...when you see their favorite TV show...when you see someone who looks like them. You pray for your person whenever their name comes to mind.

Prayer is like a blanket over your person as you lift them to God. The Bible says our prayers have great power. When you promise to pray for someone, pray for them often!

EARS TO HEAR BETTER

Don't just listen to God's word. You must do what it says. Otherwise, you are only fooling yourselves. James 1:22 (NLT)

Do you ever wonder what it would be like to hear God speak? If people had elephant ears, could they hear God better?

You may not hear God's real voice, but you can feel God's presence and His direction in a real way. You can do some things to help you hear what God is trying to tell you.

Is it easier to hear what someone is saying in a quiet place, or where there is a party going on? It's the same when you listen to God. When you calm down, take a deep breath, and turn off the TV or music, then you're more likely to understand what God wants you to know.

Sometimes hearing God better means closing your mouth. You may be telling God everything you want help with, but you aren't spending any time listening!

When you pray today, don't talk so much. Listen. You won't even need jumbo elephant ears! Just listen with your heart.

EGGSHELL PRAYERS

Make allowance for each other's faults, and forgive anyone who offends you. Remember, the Lord forgave you. Colossians 3:13 (NLT)

When someone hurts our feelings, we are quick to talk about how others offended us or spoiled the relationship. We talk, talk, talk like there is no solution.

The solution is forgiveness, but forgiving others or asking for forgiveness ourselves is never easy. We don't like to talk about things we know we should do but aren't doing.

When we refuse to forgive someone, it's like having an egg with a broken shell. Something is not right. The relationship is not how it is supposed to be. An unforgiving attitude breaks families and friends apart. Not forgiving others can make a big mess!

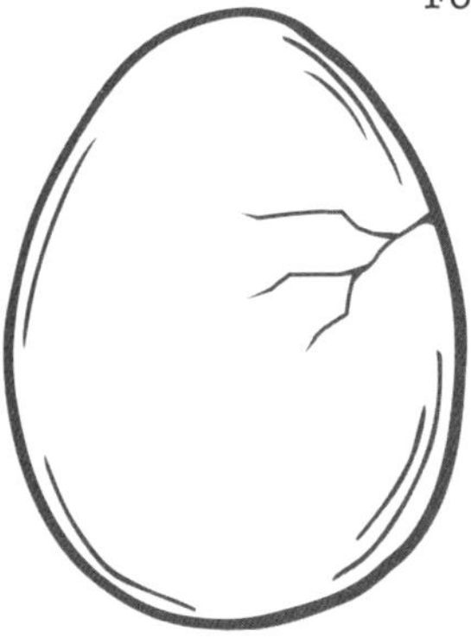

Forgiveness...where you clean up the relationship and put the wrong in the past never to bring it up again...takes God's power. It takes prayer power! Who do you need to forgive? God will give you the words and the tender heart.

ENCOURAGEMENT PRAYERS

*Encourage each other and build each other up,
just as you are already doing.*
1 Thessalonians 5:11 (NLT)

What does "encouragement" mean to you? Many times, that is what people need most.

People need encouragement when:

- They are afraid of what they have to do.
- They are getting ready to try something new.
- They have to talk to someone about a problem.
- They have a big game or a major test.
- They need to ask someone to forgive them.

Our prayers can encourage others. God can be with them when we can't. Remind people that you are praying for them. You can do that through an email, phone call, text, or written note. That will make your prayers even more encouraging!

What can you do today to encourage someone?

I'M PRAYING FOR YOU!

FIVE FINGER PRAYER

Even there your hand will guide me, your right hand will hold me fast. Psalm 139:10 (NIV)

When you need ideas for what to pray about, you have a prayer guide right at the end of your arm! Hold your hand so your thumb is almost at your mouth and your pinkie is away from you. Use each finger as a reminder to pray for specific people.

Thumb—Your thumb is closest to your face. Pray for the people who are closest to you like your family and friends.

Index Finger—People who teach you sometimes point their finger at you. Pray for your teachers at school and at church, your coaches, instructors, and pastors.

Middle Finger—This is your tallest finger. It stands out above the others. Pray for the leaders, in your country and in your church.

Ring Finger—Did you know that your ring finger is your weakest finger? Pray for people who are weak or sick, have lost a loved one, are orphaned, or are homeless.

Pinkie Finger—Your pinkie finger is farthest from your face Pray that people in far-away lands will come to know Jesus.

FULLY COMMITTED PRAYER

The eyes of the Lord *search the whole earth in order to strengthen those whose hearts are fully committed to him.* 2 Chronicles 16:9 (NLT)

What does it mean to be fully committed to God? It means that you give God everything, every moment, every action, and every thought. When you're fully committed, you go to God for help with every decision. There is nothing in your life that doesn't involve Him. Wow!

What a different life each of us would have if we could say that we are fully committed to God. Can you name some people of faith in the Bible who were fully committed? Read Hebrews 11 to learn more about some people of amazing faith!

Pray that God will show you how you can be more fully committed to Him.

GOD'S TIMING PRAYER

As the heavens are higher than the earth, so are my ways higher than your ways and my thoughts than your thoughts. Isaiah 55:9 (NIV)

When you pray, are you a little disappointed when God doesn't give you an answer right away?

When their brother, Lazarus, was sick, Mary and Martha expected Jesus to come right away. (Read John 11:1–44.) Instead, Jesus waited three days before going to Lazarus. When Jesus arrived, Mary said, "Lord, if You had been here, my brother would not have died." Mary couldn't think past her timing. She wanted Jesus to come NOW. Mary and Martha thought of God's power in their terms. In their minds, the only way God could work a miracle and show His power would be to heal Lazarus right away. But our God is full of options we can't even imagine.

God always answers our prayers. He doesn't see our name pop up on His phone and say, "Oh, I don't want to talk to them. I don't want to answer their question." God just knows what is best for us and what will cause us to give Him glory. Our lives should be about doing anything we can to bring God glory...and that means trusting Him and His timing.

GRAB IT PRAYER

If the Son sets you free, you will be free indeed. John 8:36 (NIV)

God wants us to be free from the wrong things in our lives, so people can see Jesus in us.

What do you need to be free of?

- Have you let your mouth say things it shouldn't? Do you need to be set free from a filthy mouth?
- Have you been bullying other kids? Do you need to be set free from feeling like you're "big and bad"?
- Are you too comfortable with telling little lies? Do you need to be set free from lying?
- Are you full of anger at your parents? Do you need to be set free from your awful anger?

Write down what grabs hold of your life—something you keep doing even though you know it displeases God. No matter what you write on the paper, God has the power to free you from it, if that's what your heart wants. Take some time now to talk with God about that.

HANDLE WITH PRAYER

Don't worry about anything; instead, pray about everything. Tell God what you need, and thank him for all he has done. Then you will experience God's peace. Philippians 4:6-7 (NLT)

Have you ever had a bruise? Maybe you turned a corner too quickly and rammed your arm into the door. Or you were wrestling on the floor and hit your knee on the coffee table. Or you were riding your bike and took a tumble.... Yeah, those bruises were everywhere!

A bruise leaves a mark, and it hurts. Those are physical bruises, and we can see those. Other bruises are on the inside where we can't see. How do your feelings get bruised? Does your spirit ever get bruised?

My feelings get bruised when:

- Someone calls me a name.
- I don't get picked for a team.
- Mom or Dad yells at me.
- I'm not good at something.
- I forget my lines in front of an audience.
- Everyone yells at me for missing a play in the game.

Ask God to help heal any bruised feelings you have.

HIGH AND LIFTED UP PRAYER

In the year that King Uzziah died I saw also the LORD sitting upon a throne, high and lifted up, and his train filled the temple.
Isaiah 6:1 (KJV)

Can you imagine what it would be like to see God sitting on His throne? Isaiah got a glimpse of what it was like, and he described it in Isaiah 6:1. He said that God was "high and lifted up." Isn't that a wonderful thing to think about?

In our minds and hearts, God should always be "high and lifted up." When you lift your chin and look to the sky, you can imagine the angels singing "high and lifted up." Everything we do should send a message to everyone around us that we want to lift God high. We do that with our praise, the way we live, and our worship and prayer.

Write down some things to praise God for. Then, for each thing on your list, pray: "God, I praise You today for __________________. May You be high and lifted up!"

HURRIED PRAYERS

Great is the Lord*! He is most worthy of praise! No one can measure his greatness.* Psalm 145:3 (NLT)

How do you think God feels when we rush through our prayer time? God doesn't want us to pray because someone else told us what to say. He doesn't want us to cram talking with Him into a designated amount of time. God wants us to talk to Him from our heart.

When we hurry through our time with someone so we can go somewhere else, that person probably doesn't feel very cared for. Wherever we're going or whatever we're going to do must be a lot more enjoyable or important. If all we give to God is hurried time, then God gets the message that He isn't special to us or worthy of our love and time.

What's the condition of your heart? Are you sad? Excited? Worried? Take a deep breath. Don't look at the clock. Just relax. Tell God what's on your mind. Then listen to what He is telling you. That's praying the way God wants you to talk with Him!

"IN REMEMBRANCE OF ME" PRAYER

Do this in remembrance of me. Luke 22:19 (NIV)

Jesus shared the ceremony of communion with His disciples. (Read Luke 22:14–23.) When we eat the bread and drink the juice, we remember Jesus' body and blood. We remember He died on the cross for us.

When you pray, tell Jesus some of the special things you want to remember about Him.

- I want to remember that You died for me.
- I want to remember that You love me.
- I want to remember that You want me to serve You all the time.

Dear God,
I want to remember how wonderful it was that You sent Your Son for me. Each time I eat bread, drink juice, or sing a praise song, I want to remember how awesome You are and how important You are in my life. Thank You for doing for me what I couldn't do for myself.
Amen.

LAY DOWN YOUR TREASURE

Where your treasure is, there your heart will be also. Luke 12:34 (NIV)

What is your most treasured possession? What would you be most upset about if it was destroyed or stolen? What would make you cry if it was suddenly taken from you?

When Jesus left heaven and came to earth, He gave up His most treasured possession. Can you imagine leaving heaven to do anything? No place is better than heaven! But Jesus came to give Himself as a payment for our sins. What Jesus gave was bigger than anything we treasure.

Mark 12:41–44 talks about a woman who gave her last two coins. She gave everything she had. Another woman in Mark 14:3–9 poured expensive perfume on Jesus. She gave a valuable, precious, personal treasure. But Jesus' gift to us was bigger than either of those gifts.

Ask God to help you think about your possessions in the right way. You can say a simple prayer like this:

God,
I give You my treasure. Help me not to get caught up in the things I have. I want You to be my most precious treasure.
Amen.

LEFT HAND, RIGHT HAND PRAYER

I will praise you as long as I live, lifting up my hands to you in prayer. Psalm 63:4 (NLT)

Do you remember the story of the 12 spies who went into the Promised Land? (Read Numbers 13.) All 12 men saw the same things, but they perceived them differently. Joshua and Caleb trusted God and wanted to take the land. The other 10 men were afraid and lacked the faith to move forward.

Hold out your hands. Your left hand stands for Caleb and Joshua. Your right hand stands for the 10 spies.

- If you see the bad side of things, put your right hand in your lap (10 spies). If you see the good side, put your left hand in your lap (Caleb and Joshua).
- If your faith is weak, put your right hand in your lap. If your faith is strong, put your left hand in your lap.
- If you talk people out of doing what God wants, put your right hand in your lap. If you encourage people to follow God, put your left hand in your lap.

When our hands are face down, they can't hold anything. When our hands are turned upward, they can be filled.

- If you want to speak God's words into someone else's life, turn your hands so they can be filled.
- If you want to have a strong faith in God like Caleb and Joshua, turn your hands so they can be filled.
- If you want to encourage people to follow God, then turn your hands so they can be filled.

MERCY PRAYER

Answer me when I call to you, O God who declares me innocent. Free me from my troubles. Have mercy on me and hear my prayer. Psalm 4:1 (NLT)

God could have punished us for our sins and sent us away from His presence forever. Instead, God showed us mercy (His compassion and forgiveness) when He sent His Son to save us from our sins. If you have accepted Jesus as your Savior, this prayer will remind you of that wonderful gift. If you haven't made that decision yet, this prayer will help you to do that. We all need God's mercy.

As you read this prayer, the meaning of each phrase is in parentheses.

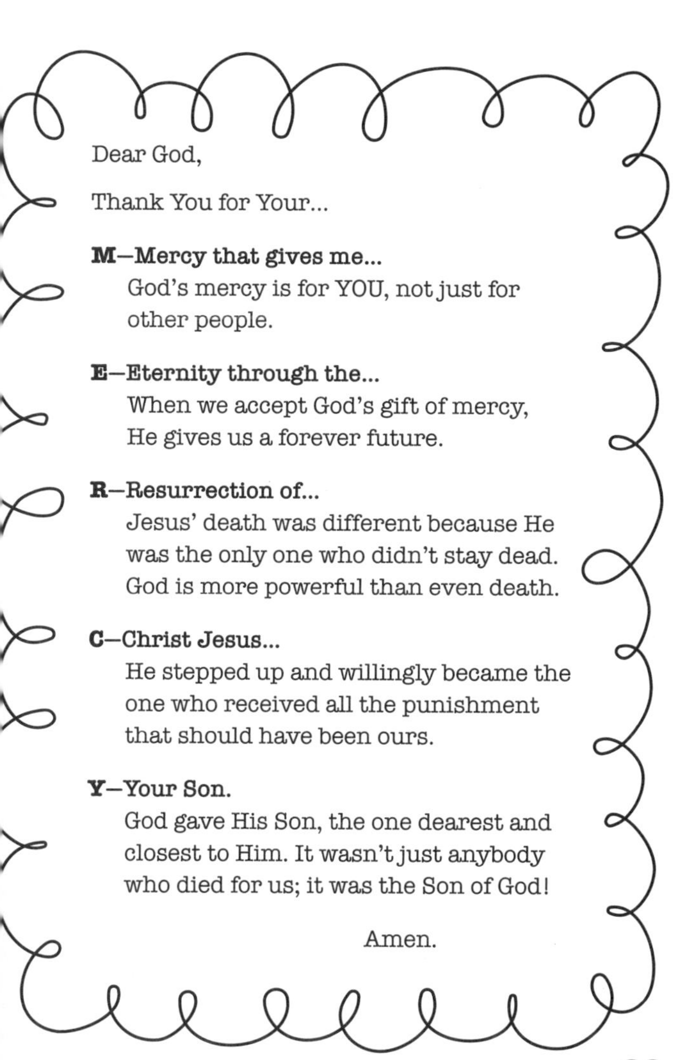

Dear God,

Thank You for Your...

M—Mercy that gives me...
God's mercy is for YOU, not just for other people.

E—Eternity through the...
When we accept God's gift of mercy, He gives us a forever future.

R—Resurrection of...
Jesus' death was different because He was the only one who didn't stay dead. God is more powerful than even death.

C—Christ Jesus...
He stepped up and willingly became the one who received all the punishment that should have been ours.

Y—Your Son.
God gave His Son, the one dearest and closest to Him. It wasn't just anybody who died for us; it was the Son of God!

Amen.

NOT-SO-INDEPENDENT PRAYER

Seek his will in all you do, and he will show you which path to take. Proverbs 3:6 (NLT)

What are some things you know how to do by yourself? What are some things you need help with?

Sometimes in life we may think we don't need God's help. Maybe we think we have just a little problem, and we're sure we can figure it out on our own.

Do we really want to do everything on our own?
God promises to be with us and to go with us through everything in our lives. He knows better than anyone else how to work through problems and how to succeed at the projects we attempt. God knows what's good for us and what we should run away from. Asking for God's help is always wise, even when we think we can do things by ourselves.

Fill in the blanks in these prayers with your own words.

Dear God, I welcome You to help me, even when I think I can ____________________ on my own.

Dear God, I invite You to help me when I don't know how to ____________________.

OBSTACLES PRAYER

In this world you will have trouble.
But take heart! I have overcome the world.
John 16:33 (NIV)

Paul was being taken to Rome as a prisoner. (Read Acts 27.) A terrible storm came and was about to tear the ship apart. An angel of the Lord told Paul how to save the people on board. Everyone had to stay with the ship until the right time. At Paul's signal, everyone would swim for shore. Men who couldn't swim grabbed wood from the shipwreck and floated to shore. Not a single man died.

What obstacle are you having a difficult time with? We all have problems sometimes, and we need God's help. Prayer is like one of those pieces of wood that kept the men afloat in the sea. Prayer is one of the ways God gives us to survive difficult times.

Lord,
I know I will have difficult times in my life. I know You want me to be a survivor. So, right now I am bringing You my obstacle and asking for Your help. Please help me with ____________________. I don't want to quit, run away, or panic. I want to be a survivor with Your help.
Amen.

PALM BRANCH PRAYER

> *The crowds that went ahead of him and those that followed shouted, "Hosanna to the Son of David! Blessed is he who comes in the name of the Lord!"*
> Matthew 21:9 (NIV)

Isn't it great when people say something really nice to you...and that's all they wanted to say?

They didn't want anything from you. They didn't want to complain. They just wanted to tell you something they appreciate about you or point out something you did that was good.

We can pray and just tell God what we appreciate about Him. No asking. No complaining. Just praising!

Just like the people in the crowd shouted out "Hosanna!" when Jesus passed by on His way to Jerusalem, we can shout out our praise to Jesus. What words would you use to praise Jesus? Make your words simple, like words that could be heard in a crowd. Offer praise to Jesus because of who He is and not just for what He has done or given to you.

PIT PRAYERS

> *You meant evil against me, but God meant it for good...to keep many people alive.*
> Genesis 50:20 (NASB)

So many awful things happened to Joseph. (Read Genesis 37–50.) First, his brothers threw him into a cistern—a pit where rainwater gathered. Then they sold him as a slave to some merchants. In Egypt, Joseph was thrown in prison for something he didn't do.

Through it all, Joseph remained faithful to God. He worked hard no matter what happened, and he lived a godly life. All those "pit"-iful things put him in a place where something wonderful could happen. Pharaoh made him second in command of all Egypt. When the drought came and his brothers came to buy grain, Joseph was able to help them.

We have "pit"-iful situations sometimes too. Bad things happen, and we don't understand why. Write down a difficult time you are having right now. As you throw your paper in the trash, pray: "God, I know You can take my bad situation and turn it into something good."

POUNDING PRAYER

Do nothing out of selfish ambition or vain conceit. Rather, in humility value others above yourselves. Philippians 2:3 (NIV)

When bighorn sheep have a conflict, do you know what they do? They ram each other in the head! Hopefully, we can deal with our conflicts without butting heads. Sometimes when we're not seeing eye-to-eye with someone, a fight breaks out. Even if you don't throw a punch, you're still not thinking nice thoughts about that person.

Pound your fist into your other palm. Really pound it! That represents a conflict. When you're in conflict, you get all tense and your fingers form a fist. Now lay your flat hand against the palm you just hit. That's better! When we open our hands, we're ready to set things aside, ready to receive, and ready to give.

Conflict happens when you want your way, and you're being stubborn. It happens when someone insults you or calls you a name. It happens when you think you're better, stronger, or smarter than another person.

God has ways of helping us with our conflict.

As you say these prayers, pound your fist to represent the conflict. Lay your flat hand against your other hand to show how God wants you to handle conflict.

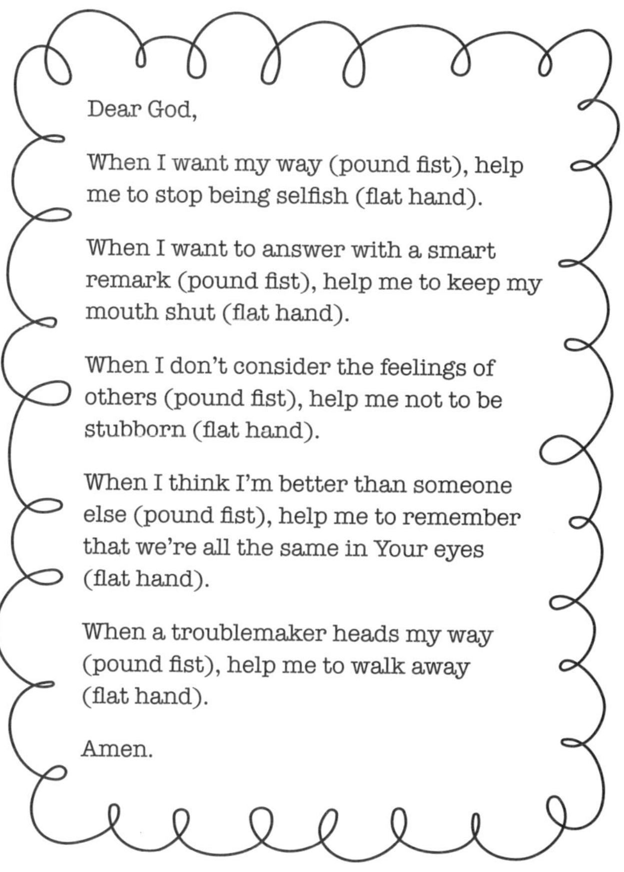

Dear God,

When I want my way (pound fist), help me to stop being selfish (flat hand).

When I want to answer with a smart remark (pound fist), help me to keep my mouth shut (flat hand).

When I don't consider the feelings of others (pound fist), help me not to be stubborn (flat hand).

When I think I'm better than someone else (pound fist), help me to remember that we're all the same in Your eyes (flat hand).

When a troublemaker heads my way (pound fist), help me to walk away (flat hand).

Amen.

PRAY FOR YOUR PASTOR

Pray also for me, that whenever I speak, words may be given me so that I will fearlessly make known the mystery of the gospel.... Pray that I may declare it fearlessly, as I should.
Ephesians 6:19-20 (NIV)

In the Bible, Moses was the main leader of the Israelite people. His responsibility was to guide and teach the people according to what God told him to do. A church has a leader too—a pastor. His responsibility is to lead the people of the congregation according to what God tells him to do.

Here are some things to pray for your pastor. Pray that:

- He will preach God's Word.
- He will understand the Bible.
- He will listen to the Holy Spirit.
- He will be kept safe and healthy.
- He will sleep well at night.
- He will enjoy time with his family.
- He will always speak with God's wisdom.

PRAYER AGAINST TEMPTATION

Keep watch and pray, so that you will not give in to temptation. Matthew 26:41 (NLT)

When Jesus went to the wilderness for 40 days, Satan tempted Him there. Jesus fasted and had not had anything to eat for 40 days. How would you feel if you had gone that long without eating?

When you're hungry, you don't want to deal with difficult situations like the temptations Satan threw at Jesus. But Jesus had some ways to defend Himself. Jesus did not give in, even when Satan offered Him a way to have fresh bread for His empty belly. Jesus knew His stomach was not as important as staying true to God.

Jesus used the Word of God to beat Satan. Jesus had the Scriptures in His heart and mind for strength. Jesus told Satan to get out of His sight. Jesus walked away from Satan's yapping.

This prayer will help you stand strong against temptation.

Dear God,
Thank You that Jesus beat Satan's temptations. Help me to do the same. Help me not to give in to Satan's lies. Help me to remember Bible verses that will make me strong. Help me to walk away from a tempting situation when I need to. Help me to know when Satan is trying to trick me.

Amen.

PRAY LIKE MOSES

When Moses heard this, he fell facedown.
Numbers 16:4 (NIV)

When Korah rebelled against Moses' leadership, the Bible tells us how Moses reacted. (Read Numbers 16.) Moses fell face down on the ground. He wasn't playing dead. He was praying! That's because Moses was a godly leader, and godly leaders go to God in prayer as soon as there is a problem...not as a last resort when nothing else works.

Moses knew he needed to pray RIGHT NOW. In a desperate situation, people who are following God's plan go to God. That's what godly people do. Moses didn't just bow his head and close his eyes. No, he threw himself on the ground and buried his head in his hands because this problem was so huge. Even his body was saying, "You are big, God. I am just your lowly servant. I need Your help!"

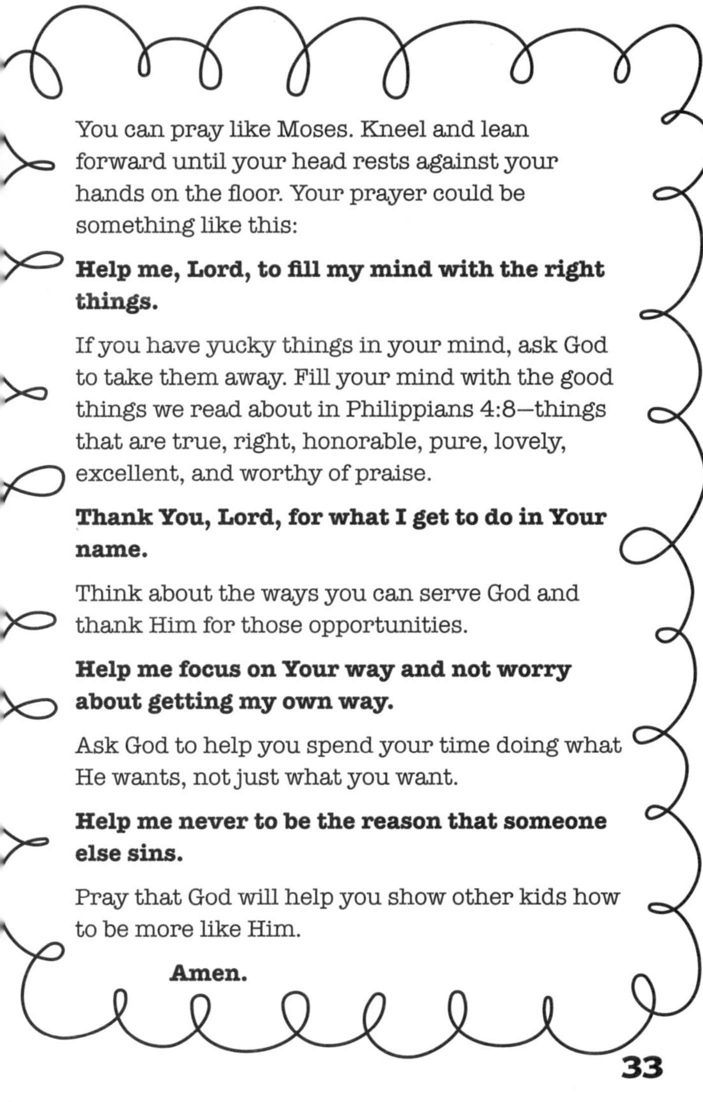

You can pray like Moses. Kneel and lean forward until your head rests against your hands on the floor. Your prayer could be something like this:

Help me, Lord, to fill my mind with the right things.

If you have yucky things in your mind, ask God to take them away. Fill your mind with the good things we read about in Philippians 4:8—things that are true, right, honorable, pure, lovely, excellent, and worthy of praise.

Thank You, Lord, for what I get to do in Your name.

Think about the ways you can serve God and thank Him for those opportunities.

Help me focus on Your way and not worry about getting my own way.

Ask God to help you spend your time doing what He wants, not just what you want.

Help me never to be the reason that someone else sins.

Pray that God will help you show other kids how to be more like Him.

Amen.

PRAYER EGGS

I am praying to you because I know you will answer, O God. Bend down and listen as I pray.
Psalm 17:6 (NLT)

When Jesus was in the Garden of Gethsemane, He poured out His heart to His Father in heaven. (Read Matthew 26:36–46.) How awful it must have been to know He was going to be nailed to a cross and killed. But still, Jesus prayed and obeyed God's will.

On the next page, you will find some short prayers to use during Holy Week or any time of the year. You can write them on slips of paper, cut them apart, and put them in plastic Easter eggs. If you don't have eggs, use a small jar.

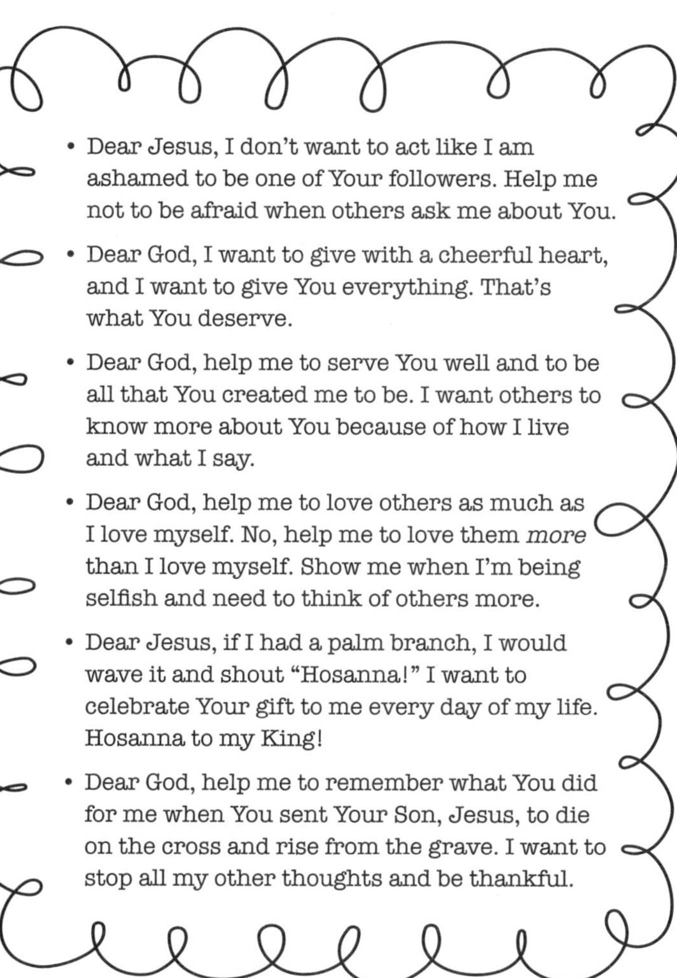

- Dear Jesus, I don't want to act like I am ashamed to be one of Your followers. Help me not to be afraid when others ask me about You.
- Dear God, I want to give with a cheerful heart, and I want to give You everything. That's what You deserve.
- Dear God, help me to serve You well and to be all that You created me to be. I want others to know more about You because of how I live and what I say.
- Dear God, help me to love others as much as I love myself. No, help me to love them *more* than I love myself. Show me when I'm being selfish and need to think of others more.
- Dear Jesus, if I had a palm branch, I would wave it and shout "Hosanna!" I want to celebrate Your gift to me every day of my life. Hosanna to my King!
- Dear God, help me to remember what You did for me when You sent Your Son, Jesus, to die on the cross and rise from the grave. I want to stop all my other thoughts and be thankful.

PURE HEART PRAYER

How can a young person stay pure?
By obeying your word. Psalm 119:9 (NLT)

Do you stay mad at people for a long time and for no good reason?

Do you think mean things about certain people?

Do you do certain things so that others will notice you and like you?

Do you sometimes consider yourself better than other people?

What we think on the inside matters, even if we don't say mean things or act the wrong way on the outside. We can keep our heart pure by keeping God and His Word front and center in our minds.

Spend some time praying about what you can do to keep your heart pure.

Lord, when I

_______________________,

help me to remember that You want me to keep my heart pure. Amen.

RED CORD PRAYER

> *A person standing alone can be attacked and defeated, but two can stand back-to-back and conquer. Three are even better, for a triple-braided cord is not easily broken.*
> Ecclesiastes 4:12 (NLT)

When Rahab hid the spies in the flax on her roof, she showed great courage. (Read Joshua 2.) Even though she was not an Israelite, she recognized God's power and believed the God of the Israelites was the One True God. Rahab took a huge risk of being punished severely when she defended the spies instead of turning them in.

As a reward for her courage, Rahab's household would be protected when the city was attacked if she tied a red cord in her window.

Courage is what you need when you're going into unfamiliar territory, when you are trying something completely new. You need courage when you are in a situation where you are different from the people and events around you.

Think about a time when you have needed courage. Tie a red string around your finger as a reminder to pray. With God beside you, your courage will not be broken.

WHEN YOU FEEL WEAK PRAYER

The Holy Spirit helps us in our weakness.
Romans 8:26 (NLT)

Do you ever feel like you just can't do something? Have you ever felt like your teacher or coach picked the wrong person when he or she chose you? We all feel weak when we don't live up to what we think others expect of us or what we expect of ourselves. We also feel weak when we have something in our lives that we just can't seem to get past.

Paul felt like that. Apparently, some kind of nagging illness constantly bothered Paul. He felt weak. But 2 Corinthians 12:9 (NLT) tells us that Paul gained strength when he realized what God's response to his weakness was. God said, "My grace is all you need. My power works best in weakness." Paul goes on to say, "So now I am glad to boast about my weaknesses, so that the power of Christ can work through me."

We all need to pray about our weaknesses. We need to hand them over to God and claim His grace and power. When you attack your weakness with prayer, the power of Christ can work through you, just like it did with Paul.

STRENGTH TRAINING PRAYER

Pray continually, give thanks in all circumstances; for this is God's will for you in Christ Jesus. 1 Thessalonians 5:17-18 (NIV)

Have you ever seen someone work out with weights? To grow big muscles, you must lift a lot of weights—heavy weights—over and over every day. Little by little, the bodybuilder's muscles get stronger. We can strengthen our prayer muscles too by praying continually, over and over every day.

Praying continually helps us develop a strong faith. That means praying at times other than right before bed or before a meal. When you continually pray, it strengthens your relationship with God, and that strengthens your faith and commitment to Him.

How do your arms feel when you lift weights? A little tingly? Tired? When you first start exercising, your muscles aren't used to all that action. But each day they will get stronger. Prayer is kind of like that too. When you make praying a holy habit, you won't even notice that you're praying about everything that happens in your life. It's just the natural thing to do because you've strengthened your praying muscles.

TALENTED TALENTS PRAYER

We continually ask God to fill you with the knowledge of his will…so that you may live a life worthy of the Lord and please him in every way.
Colossians 1:9-10 (NIV)

What are you good at—*really* good at? Do you play the guitar well? Are you great at math? Do you take care of plants so they are healthy and strong? Can you run fast? Are you able to help younger kids? Do other people tell you that you are good at something?

God gives us special talents, so we can use them for His Kingdom. Can you use your talent to help bring people to Jesus?

In Luke 19:11-27, Jesus tells a parable about a ruler who gave three servants some money. Then the ruler went away. Two of the servants used the money to make more. The third servant buried his and didn't use it. When the ruler returned, he was happy with the two servants who had used the money they were given, but he was upset with the man who buried the money he was given. In fact, the ruler was so upset that he took the money away from the third man completely. What do you think that tells us about the talents God gives each of us?

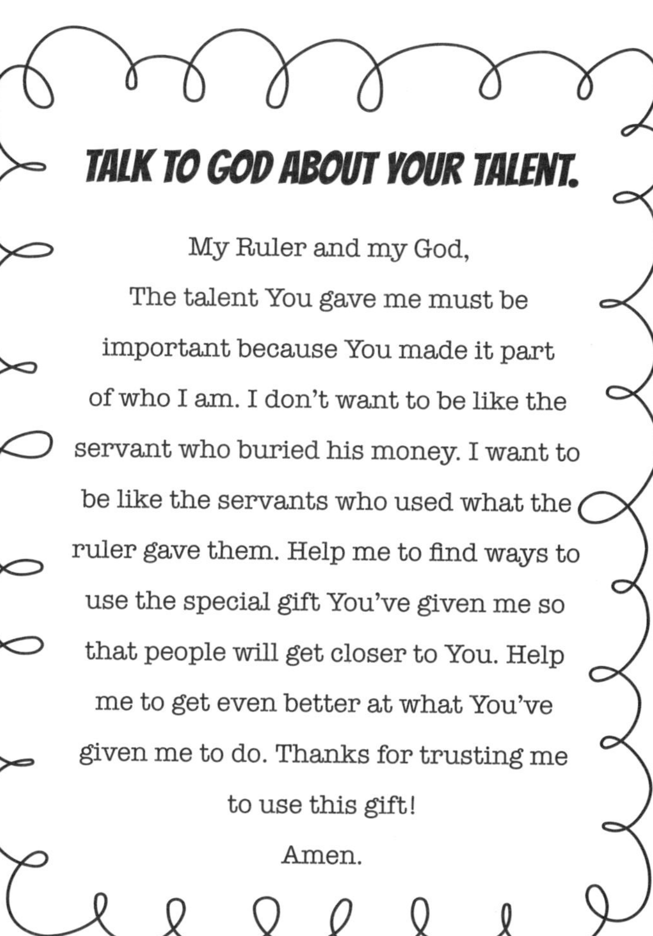

TALK TO GOD ABOUT YOUR TALENT.

My Ruler and my God,
The talent You gave me must be important because You made it part of who I am. I don't want to be like the servant who buried his money. I want to be like the servants who used what the ruler gave them. Help me to find ways to use the special gift You've given me so that people will get closer to You. Help me to get even better at what You've given me to do. Thanks for trusting me to use this gift!
Amen.

THRESHING FLOOR PRAYER

I prayed to the L*ORD, and he answered me. He freed me from all my fears.* Psalm 34:4 (NLT)

In Judges 6, the Bible tells us that the Midianites were causing the Israelites terrible trouble. God sent an angel to Gideon, who was hiding down in a winepress to thresh wheat. At that moment, Gideon received his order from God about what he was to do.

God had chosen Gideon to lead the fight against the Midianites. There on the threshing floor, the angel assured Gideon that God would be with him, and that gave Gideon new hope for the future of the Israelite people. The threshing floor is where Gideon asked the Lord questions and made his decision to obey God's command.

Maybe you need to make a decision or a promise to God. Your threshing floor can be any place where you ask God questions.

What do you want to ask God? Here are some sample questions to get you started.

- Do you wonder why bad things have happened to you or your family? Ask God your questions.
- Do you wonder how God could ever use you? Ask God your questions.
- Do you think you are too weak, too little, or too young to do what God asks you to do? Ask God your questions.
- Do you need to make a promise to worship God with all your heart? Make a new commitment to God. He can handle your questions.

TUG-O-WAR PRAYER

Love your enemies and pray for those who persecute you. Matthew 5:44 (NIV)

When you are in conflict with someone, you feel like you are being pulled in different directions. The other person doesn't understand why you want what you want. The other person doesn't understand why you have a certain opinion. Maybe the other person doesn't understand why you do things the way you do. Conflict doesn't feel good.

When you play tug-o-war, two people or teams pull in opposite directions. They definitely aren't going the same direction. When we don't get along with someone we love, we feel like we are being pulled apart. Those situations car tear up a relationship.

Is there someone you're in conflict with right now? Pray this sentence prayer:

Dear God, help me to find ways to get along with ________________(insert name). Amen.

Wait quietly and write down any ways that God brings to mind.

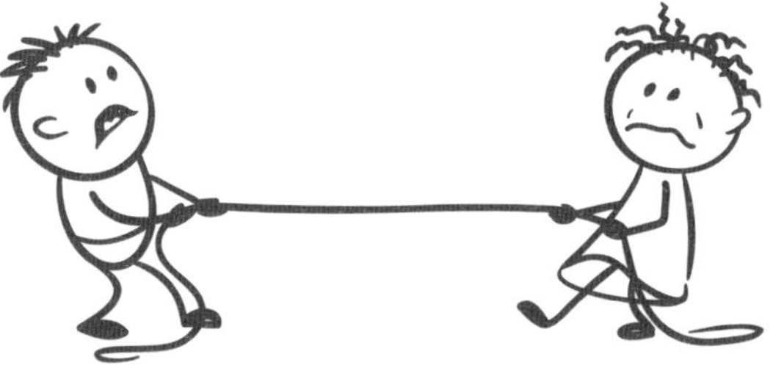

WET WIPE PRAYER

Create in me a clean heart, O God; and renew a right spirit within me. Psalm 51:10 (KJV)

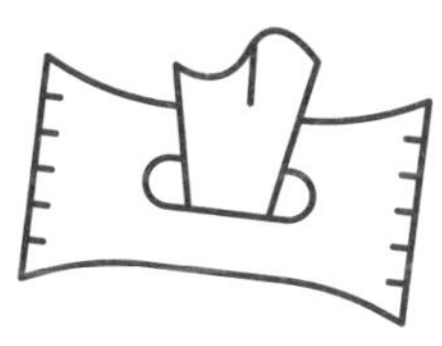

/hat do you do with a wet wipe? It's eally good at cleaning up a mess! 'ou can use one to clean muddy .ands, dirty little baby bottoms, a ticky steering wheel, or the push ar on a grocery cart.

. wet wipe cleans all kinds of things on the outside, but ; can't clean you on the inside. It reminds you of all the hings that have been dirty but aren't anymore. A wet /ipe can become a symbol for all the dirty things that are .ow clean.

'ind a marker and a wet wipe (or a damp paper towel).

f you have accepted Jesus as your Savior, write on your /et wipe something simple like "God made me clean."

f there is a "messy" or stressful situation in your home r at school right now, write a short prayer about that on 'our wet wipe.

f God has already helped you with a messy situation, /rite a thank you prayer on your wet wipe.

:nd your prayer time with, "Thank You, God, for cleaning ıs up on the inside." Then rub the wet wipe between your .ands to clean the outside!

WINDOW PRAYER

Daniel...went home to his upstairs room where the window opened toward Jerusalem. Three times a day he got down on his knees and prayed.
Daniel 6:10 (NIV)

King Nebuchadnezzar made a law stating that for 30 days everyone in his kingdom could pray only to him. (Read Daniel 6.) No other prayers and no other gods were allowed. If anyone chose to go against the law, that person would be thrown into the lions' den.

Daniel was a devoted believer in the One True God. When he prayed, Daniel was not ashamed. He didn't care what other people thought of him. He only knew that he loved God so much. Three times a day, Daniel prayed right by his window where everyone could see—even though it was against the law to do so!

Write the word PRAY on a sheet of paper and tape it to your bedroom window. Every time you see the word, think abou how Daniel prayed three times a day. Remember to pray often and tell Go how much you love Him.

WISDOM PRAYER

If any of you lacks wisdom, let him ask of God, who gives to all generously and without reproach, and it will be given to him. James 1:5 (NASB)

/hat would you ask God for if He said you could have one ning...anything you wanted?

n 1 Kings 3:1–15, the Bible tells us about King Solomon's ream. In that dream God told Solomon that he could ame anything, and God would give it to him. Wouldn't nat be cool!

e wasn't sure he was wise enough to be a good king. So, ing Solomon asked God for wisdom.

'isdom isn't just for kings. It's for us too! James 1:5 says nat if we lack wisdom, we should ask God for it. And what ill God do? He will give it...generously...more and more.

s there a situation in your fe right now where you need ore wisdom so you can andle it the way God wants ou to? You can ask God for ore wisdom, just like King olomon did!

WIPE OUT JEALOUSY PRAYER

I have learned the secret of being content in any and every situation.... I can do all this through him who gives me strength. Philippians 4:12-13 (NIV)

Each time you are thankful to God, you chase away jealousy. You can't be truly thankful and jealous of others at the same time. Jealous feelings leave when we are content with what we have.

Jealousy makes you unhappy. You may fall into the trap of thinking that if you could just have the next thing, you'd be happy. Maybe you've thought something like: "I am so jealous of those middle school students. If only I could be in middle school, then I would be happy!" Then you might get to middle school and think you'll only be happy when you get to high school. The cycle could continue through your whole life! Your life could turn out sad because you were always thinking about how happy other people must be and wishing you could be like them.

Today, God can set you free from jealousy. He can change your heart if you put your focus on Him. Pray for people you may be jealous of. Thank God for the blessings He gives everyone. Remember the good things God has given to you! Ask God to replace your jealous heart with a grateful one.